Business (Head) Transformation

Challenge Your Mindset, Management Processes
for
Sustainable Business Profitability & Growth

S. GANESH BABU

Title	: Business (Head) Transformation
Author	: S. Ganesh Babu
Mobile	: +91 90259 33666
Email	: ganesh@winningmindssolutions.com
Copyright	: Author
Published by	: Winning Minds Solutions, Pondicherry
First edition	: 2017
Price	: ₹ 200

© Ganesh babu. All rights reserved.

This book helps
small, emerging medium size business
promoters / CEOs / heads of the organizations
to improve business profitability and growth
so that
they can maximize their personal productivity and quality
of life.

I dedicate this book to
SME business heads
who are striving for excellence in their business.

Advance Praise for the Book

This book reflects the culmination of knowledge and experience in guiding SMEs. Knowledge is information but transforming the information into skill is an art. Shri. Ganesh Babu has taken the pain to pen his experience and knowledge.

This book mirrors "Rudimentary knowledge explained in a simple and understandable way to have a profound impact on SMEs".

This book is useful and we strongly recommend it for the SMEs.

Essae Chandran Institute, Bangalore, India

Once again, I am amazed at the insights Ganesh Babu has gained and the simple manner in which he has explained the important aspects. The book is also laid out thoughtfully, by explaining the mindset required for business growth, then explaining the processes to be driven through the organization to scale up. The checklist is a good ready reckoner and a practitioner will appreciate this. Overall, it is easy to read, interesting and holds the reader's attention and one can easily make out that the author has actually practiced what he talks about in the book.

God bless Ganesh Babu

B.L.P Simha, Senior Vice President (Global Operations), Wipro Infrastructure Engineering Limited, Bangalore, India.

The author has given prescription for sustainable business profitability and growth through his hands on experience and wide practical knowledge. This book is very simple but thought provoking.

The book is divided into four parts, starting from limiting beliefs, mindsets of leaders, summarizing the business principles, processes and practices and comprehensive checklists. He has also listed basic management concepts, tools and techniques, which will help leaders to have quick review and their applicability.

The author has emphasized the role and transformation of the business head to achieve sustainable growth of people and business. I am confident that by reading and introspecting the ideas and concepts explained in this book, leaders of SMEs and other organizations will benefit and bring about transformation of self and enhance the business performance.

I wish the readers an enriching journey towards excellence.

R.Gopu, Retired GM of TI Cycles of India, Management Consultant, Chennai, India

How an organization works is dictated by a set of experiences the people have, that drive beliefs that lead to actions that end in results. To change the results, we must not only focus on actions, but also our beliefs and experiences. So focus on beliefs, behavior, experiences that are critical for sustainable business profitability and growth.

Ganesh Babu has made a compelling and expertly made case through this book how critical small, medium size business head's beliefs, attitudes, business processes for sustainable business profitability and growth. I loved the book.

A.H.B. Narayanareddy, Senior Director-Plant Head, Whirlpool of India Limited, Pune, India.

Here is a potentially useful book for all business owners and CEOs in the MSME sector in any part of the world. It tells you very clearly, what needs to be done and why it has to be done, to put the business on the right path strategically. It also tells you how it can be done, and leaves it to the good judgment of a leader as the Where and When it can be done. The book is like a working manual for all those who wish to transform their businesses and do not have a myopic quarter-to-next-quarter approach to operations. Ideal for those who wish to enrich the people around them and give back something to the society at large."

Ashok Kumar Bhatia, Management Counselor, Thinker and writer, Pondicherry, India

At the outset that Ganesh babu's conviction that "Business Head is the one who makes or breaks a business" is commendable!

The surprising fact is that the unconscious competence of Ganesh Babu has come out in the Deming way of 1. PLAN (Minding the Mind), 2. DO (Focus Effectiveness through Business Processes), 3. CHECK (Focus on Checklists) & 4. ACT (with Wisdom provided by Established Tools & Techniques)

Most of the authors will take few concepts and describe elaborately in their books. Ganesh Babu for a change has taken all the concepts required for managing the Small, Medium & Emerging Business in Intensely Interesting and Simple way.

Alwin Toffler, the Futurologist has defined Illiterates of 21st Century as those people who cannot Learn, Unlearn & Relearn! This book prepares you to become not only literate but also an able CEO to run the business effectively!

Every entrepreneur who wants to be successful must read this book first and then start and focus on Business.

K.NAGARAJA KUMAR erstwhile Head-HR, SCSR & Improvement Initiatives at L&T Rubber Processing Machinery and currently serving Larsen & Toubro – Corporate Technical as Consultant & Head Marketing

A must read for every entrepreneur!

The author presents the very powerful concepts in a simple and easy to understand manner. While many big corporate have already many excellence initiatives underway, author has done a noble job by writing this book for helping small and medium business enterprises to pursue their excellence journey.

Prabhakaran Kuralnidhi, Head –Business Excellence, RAK Ceramics, UAE

Foreword by the Author

I would like to thank you for reading this book and your intention to buy this book shows that you are curious to improve your business profitability and growth. I assure you that this book will give you different perspectives about yourself and your business practices that are affecting business profitability and growth.

This book is the outcome of my working experience with more than 100 small- and medium-size business heads for last 21 years. I have had the opportunity to work with them on different occasions and with different roles, either as a mentor, coach, trainer, or advisor, to improve business processes, profitability, growth, and to build a performance-oriented culture. While working with them, one profound truth that I have realized is that irrespective of industry, business nature, product, manufacturing process, marketing environment and competition, *the growth of the organization primarily depends on the business head leadership style, his thinking process, and how he is guiding his team.*

A business head's mindset or beliefs about his business, people and customers drive his behavior and action. Those actions result in business performance. Also, his mindset or belief directs him to choose a set of business processes or practices on a day-to-day basis, which impacts the organizational culture, business results, and long-term growth.

In our business transformation engagements, we have witnessed that whenever the CEO or business head understands the desirable behavior gap or the business process gap and then works full heartedly along with us, the business results used to be extraordinary. In my opinion, business success factors like technology upgradation, effective capacity utilization, expanding into new markets, managing the competition, and fulfilling the customers' requirements are relatively easy tasks if the CEO or business head is a little challenging and changes his mindset, beliefs, and business processes.

I firmly believe that the *transformation of the business head is almost equal to business transformation.* Business transformation starts from an individual and that too from the head of the organization.

In the above context, I had attempted to give some perspective on the limiting beliefs and mindset that most of the small business heads have. I had outlined the solution approach to overcome the limiting beliefs and given some of the proven business principles, processes, and practices for sustainable business profitability and growth.

The awareness about business transformation is organized into *FOUR* parts.

1) The first part deals with typical limiting beliefs and mindsets of business head that affect the business growth and solutions approach to overcome the same.
2) The second part deals with some of the proven business principles, processes, and practices that will help improve the business profitability, culture, and growth.
3) The third part lists out a comprehensive business process checklist to help the business head or CEO quickly scan through their business processes and understand the gaps to achieve sustainable business growth.
4) The fourth part lists some of the basic, powerful management concepts, tools, and techniques for business transformation.

How to get the most out of this book?

✓ You may choose to read the book from the beginning or read any chapter as you wish.

- ✓ In each chapter, we discuss some perspectives about the mindset or management processes. I suggest reading them and introspect to see whether or not these perspectives apply to you/your business. If they are applicable, challenge your mindset or processes and think on implementing them.
- ✓ You may go through the business process checklist and calibrate yourself on the implementation of those processes in your organization. This awareness will fill the gap between reality and excellence.
- ✓ You may go through some of the important management concepts, tools, and techniques as these will improve your perspectives. For more learning, please get help from other resources.
- ✓ You will get the most out of this reading only by self-introspecting and implementing the right action!

You are welcome to share your feedback about the learning or you can write to me with your concerns about your organizational growth at ganesh@winningmindssolutions.com and I am happy to help.

Wishing You Excellence in Life,

S. Ganesh Babu
Founder & CEO
Business Transformation Consultant & Performance Coach
Winning Minds Solutions
India.

November 14, 2016
mail: ganesh@winningmindssolutions.com

For business and life excellence related articles, success case studies on business transformation,
please visit
www.winningmindssolutions.com

Contents

Part 1: Mindset and beliefs affect business growth and profitability   **1**

1. Growth vs. survival mindset   2
2. Our business is special   4
3. My core expertise will save the business   6
4. Relationship matters over business growth   8
5. I want quick results somehow   10
6. Difficult to initiate new ideas implementation   12
7. I am not good at math   14
8. Treating people with fixed perception   15
9. Being busy is always good for business   16
10. Emotional decision making   18
11. Too focused on people   19
12. Learn how to deal with setbacks   20

Part 2: Business processes and practices affect business growth and profitability   **21**

13. Measure everything   22
14. Discuss the performance issues in the forum   24
15. Set business goals with conviction   26
16. Invest in talent   28
17. Improve the effectiveness before investing   30
18. Be lean on the cost structure   32
19. Systematic daily management (SDM) for assuring annual growth   33
20. Do not delegate your prime responsibility to others   34

21.	Improve the effectiveness before automation	35
22.	Improve communication and create forum	36
23.	Continuous process disruption as a way of life	38
24.	Build an environment and process for employee engagement	40

Part 3: Quick checklist to calibrate your business process gap — **43**

25.	Operations management checklist	44
26.	Strategy focus checklist	46
27.	People development checklist	47
28.	Sales management checklist	48
29.	Finance management checklist	49
30.	Marketing/product development/customer focus checklist	50

Part 4: Quick overview about management concepts, tools, and techniques for business growth and profitability — **51**

Additional resources — **63**
Expression of my gratitude — **64**
About the author: Ganesh Babu — **65**

Part 1

Mindset and Beliefs

Growth vs survival mindset

As head of the organization, your belief about your business either as "growth oriented" or as "survival oriented" determines your business growth.

If you look at your business only as a profit-making motive, you tend to make a profit somehow, irrespective of adhering to processes, ethics, considering the interest of all stakeholders, and long-term sustainability of business. That is a survival mindset.

Instead, if you can change your perspective to look at the purpose of business as one to "enhance the value to all stakeholders", then that is a growth mindset. This perspective will improve your thought process toward long-term sustainable business decisions.

There are many stakeholders such as employees, customers, suppliers, banking finance institutions, promoters, the government, and society, and each has different interests or value expectations from the organization. For example, as an employee the value expectation would be better pay, learning, and growth opportunities, as customers the value expectation would be the best product or service for money, and as suppliers the value expectation would be regular orders and on-time payment. It is your prime responsibility to enhance the value to stakeholders in a sustainable basis for which sustainable wealth creation is the path.

If you have this perspective about the purpose of the business, your approach and thought process would be on building a solid foundation for process, systems, technology, and talent management, and in turn your visionary approach would be long term oriented even though sometimes you lose in the short term. That is the growth mindset of CEOs of successful organizations across the world.

Our business is special

Most of the small organization business heads think that their business or operations are unique and that they have their justification for their current level of performance. This thought process indirectly affects your learning from cross-industry experience and prevents your business to grow.

For any business, the industry classification, product, or process of conversion or customer's profile may be different, but the business objective is the same irrespective of the differences: serving the customer and creating wealth through the product or service. The key business performance indicators are almost the same across the business verticals.

If you understand this insight, you are open to learn the best practices from other business/industries and you are ready to implement any new smart initiatives to make the business more profitable and sustainable.

For example, sales per employee is one of the measures for the retail or service industry. The idea behind this measure is basically to improve employee productivity either by improvising the sales performance or optimizing human resources with reference to sales. Even if you are in the manufacturing industry, this measure can be used in shop floors as a product produced per man per day. This measure can be easily communicated to everyone in the shop floor and the intention is to optimize human resources with reference to production demand.

Hence, *treat your business as general, learn the best practices from any industries, and improve your business performance!*

My core expertise will save the business

Most small businesses remain in the same category for a longer duration due to the leader's mindset and their focus on daily routine management or spending too much time in their core functionality. Business owners are proud of their core skill competency and enjoy spending most of the time in their core functionality or micromanagement.

For example, you may have core qualification and experience in marketing, you may enjoy spending more time in the marketing function, and you are comfortable in micromanaging the marketing functions. In this process, you will be losing the big picture of managing the business growth.

Managing a business is all about balancing all aspects of marketing, development, manufacturing, people, sales, and finance management. As a business owner, you must overview all aspects of business management and ensure that you are taking the organization to the next level with your big picture perspective rather than behaving and working as functional experts.

A simple rule to remember: LEARN TO UNLEARN. Remember that the core functions competency which brought you to this level may not guarantee you to next level, as business growth requires a different set of competencies.

Hence, *focus on business development, exploring new opportunities, people development, and finance management rather than micromanaging your core functional expertise. Work as business managers rather than functional experts.*

Relationship matters over business growth

One of the dilemma most of the family-run business CEOs face during the growth stage is differentiating family relationship and business performance. While starting a business, it is normal to manage most of the activities by oneself or inducting relatives to manage key functions. During the development of a business, it might have given moral support and helped in many ways in sharing business responsibilities.

When the business is aspiring for big growth, professionalism matters with today's fast-changing customer expectations and preferences. Focused and specialized skill is required in all the functions to run the business effectively. Even if a CEO wants to run the business professionally and is to ready to step down, he is reluctant to change the position occupied by key relatives due to family bonding. In this dilemma, he continues to run the business with mediocre performance and of course the rate of growth slows down.

If you want to take business to the next level through a professional approach, ensure that you are challenging the unprofessional way of managing or old legacy system. *There is no second thought on the fact that family relationship is important and needs to be preserved. But this emotional sentiment should not be a barrier to potential business growth. Many stakeholders depend on business growth. It has to be dealt with rationally at the right time for sustaining the growth of the business. Hence, manage the growth phase professionally.*

I want quick results somehow

To be in business for the long term, one of the prerequisites is being patient. Being patient is very important in developing the people as well as seeing the result from new initiatives.

Have you heard about the *Chinese bamboo tree*? This tree is different from other trees as it does not grow in the usual fashion. While most of the trees start growing steadily over a period, this

Chinese bamboo tree does not even break through the ground for the first four years. Then on the fifth year, this tree starts to grow at an amazing growth rate. It is said that within four to five weeks' time, it grows 90 feet high. Actually, during the first four years, growth is not visible externally, but the tree has internally grown and made strong roots.

This nature's creation reflects our life. Sometimes, our life works this way. You may be working hard for your business growth for weeks, months, or even years and you may not even see much significant progress. All of a sudden, you realize a significant transformation or growth in your business results. Here, the key point is your patience to go through the process or faith on the positive outcome and perseverance in your effort makes you realize the result.

Having done all rigorous verification, you recruit new people. That means, you believe in their potential. Give some time for people to settle down, understand your organizational culture, products, processes, etc., and then start expecting the results. It takes time to adapt to a new environment and deliver results. One of the important roles of a CEO is to engage and develop the people and then demand the results.

Similarly, most of the heads tend to expect results as soon as they initiate new programs and change management initiatives. Be patient as change management initiatives require time to penetrate into people's mind to accept and start owning them.

Any new initiative or effort in business or even people development takes time to produce results. It requires patience and faith in the outcome.

Difficult to initiate new ideas

In the business or professional environment, the biggest challenge is selling our idea or believing that the idea will work. That is building a confidence within us and in others.

BUILDING CONFIDENCE IN SELF-LEVELS

Confidence cannot be built only through external stimuli like reading books, listening to motivational lectures, etc., as they build confidence momentarily and are short lived. Real confidence is built at a conscious level only by having and experiencing small success.

For example, if you want to improve your confidence on public speaking skills, you cannot immediately do it in a large crowd. Instead, you consciously experiment in a small group, take action, and taste the success. Your subconscious mind registers the successful event. The next time you are speaking in a larger group, your *mind pushes you with positive reinforcement of earlier success* and you do well. Again, the mind registers this event as a positive reinforcement. This way you can improve your confidence in public speaking.

BUILDING CONFIDENCE AT TEAM LEVEL

Similarly, if you want to build your team's confidence about any new initiative, they need to see it and believe it. Hence experiment with the initiatives in a small way, be focused, take action, achieve, and celebrate it. This positive reinforcement of success will give confidence to your team for taking higher level initiatives.

Building confidence is one of the leadership qualities and is time consuming, but it is more powerful once it is built.

Hence, the action plan is to identify the area in which you have low confidence level about any new idea, take small action, taste the success, and this small success will help you achieve more! Build confidence with small success!

I am not good at math

For successfully running the business on a sustainable basis, your market acumen and technical knowledge alone is not sufficient. You need to understand the basics of your finance.

At the end of the day, despite hard work, if CEO or Business head does not earn the profits, that would become more frustration. The reasons could be the lack of structured product costing and quoting process, pricing decisions, cost efficiency and also the lack of financial accounting and management. Also, we witness that the head of the organization delegates the entire responsibility to a lower level as he thinks managing finance is more of the statutory requirements.

You need not be professionally sound in finance management, but you need to be familiar with profit and loss, cash flow analysis, balance sheet, fundamentals of expenses, and product costing domain. Your analytical capability and questioning the cost parameters will improve the efficiency in cost management across the organization.

Hence, develop the competency on financial fundamentals!

Treating people with fixed perception

One of the struggle that most of the business head undergoes is that lack of soft skill in handling the peoples, even though one can be expert in technical and market savvy. Treating people with respect will have a huge impact on sustainable growth as well as on the winning spirit of the team.

Most of them are struggling with maintaining good relationships with colleagues, subordinates, and customers. One of the reasons could be the perception they have formed about others and approaching them with the same perception forever. However, the reality may be the opposite of the perception.

For example, you might have experienced a few irritable incidences with one of your direct reports and you have framed the perception that the person is always *"short-tempered."* Hence, you approach him every time with the same frame of mind and respond to him accordingly, however, you may miss his good qualities such as his grasping ability, communication skill, caring about people, business acumen, etc. In this process, your relationship quality is strained.

The point is that if you frame a certain perception about people and approach them with that same lens, then your quality of relationship will be to the extent of that perception. If you are flexible and start looking at the other qualities of people, the quality of the relationship as well as business results may improve.

Being busy is always good for business

Most of us have the tendency of *"being busy"* always. It can be in a professional or business environment either chasing the success after success or managing the challenges with the same approach. In this process, over a period we either become addicted to the same methodology without evaluating its effectiveness or we become so rigid in our thinking process that it leads to ignoring other aspects of the relationship, quality of execution, next level of growth, etc.

The study shows that one of the qualities successful people possess is *"being reflective"*. Frequently, they take time for themselves and evaluate what is going on around their business, what is important, what needs to be changed, etc. This reflection gives them clarity on the behavior to be dropped or adopted, the strategy to be modified or tuned, etc., for improving the quality of business.

Being busy always and running fast in the wrong direction will never help you achieve your goal. *Hence, then and there step back and reflect on your behavior and actions, and of course your performance!*

Emotional decision making

Even though we learn structured methodologies, tools, and techniques for arriving at logical decisions, decision making is one of the difficult aspects of life management. There are two situations where we face a decision-making dilemma. One is during a crisis (urgent) moment and another while making (important) personal life decisions like a child's education, switching profession, changing jobs, relocating, or even business investment decisions.

Our minds go as per the emotional urge during the moment of decision-making. Even though emotions drive our behavior, most of the time emotional decisions alone may not be the right solution. It is preferable to answer for both emotional and rational needs before taking an important life decision.

For example, if you desire to grow your business in the new market environment, look into emotional aspects such as passion, pride, fulfilling the ego, happiness, etc and also rationally evaluate your team's competency, skill level, financial strength, competition strength, gap needs to be filled, alternative plans, etc. *This balanced evaluation of both the emotional and the rational may give you the right mindset to take a decision, which gives you peace and happiness.*

Be aware of your decision-making pattern of all important life decisions, balanced with the emotional and rational approach.

Too focused on people

"There is no use talking about the problem unless you talk about the solutions" – Betty Williams

When things do not take place as expected or when there is a problem in the professional, business, or family environment, the usual tendency is to ask "who is responsible". For any problems, finding the cause is a good thing, but the moment we focus our search on the "people" factor, it likely turns out as blaming, complaining, justifying, and arguing and eventually turns into personal vengeance.

Instead, if we shift our focus on the "process" factor, we likely find improvements to fix the problem. Sometimes, the fixing process may prevent the issue permanently as well as take care of human errors.

Shifting the focus on fixing the "process" than the "people" is possible with a little bit of awareness on our intention and behavior. It is difficult but possible with practice. Any problem can be fixed through the process, and in turn the process will take care of the people factor too.

Just be aware of your reaction to the problem, shift the focus toward process.

Learn how to deal with setbacks

In a business or professional environment or sports, when something goes wrong the most affected people will be those who head the business, organization, function, or team – in other words, the captain of the team. The challenge for the captain is to bring back the confidence of all stakeholders through quick actions and more than that managing oneself emotionally to overcome the setback.

When we go through successful people's life stories, some common patterns emerge in their thought process and approach in dealing with setbacks.

1. They use to feel gifted to lead a team either as captain or as owner of the business. They see the position as a responsibility. They internally feel and believe that if they are blessed with such a privilege, they will also be blessed to overcome any setback. It is more about taking the setback as part of the divine play to make them strong.
2. They strongly believe that failures are acceptable. This reflection protects them from self-sabotage and think of a way forward.
3. They deeply spend time with themselves to introspect the causes and mistakes they made. They critically evaluate the assumptions, decision-making process, management style behaviors, etc.
4. They are quick to come out with an alternate plan and put into action.
5. They have a single-minded focus on the execution till they see the result.

It is not a problem of falling. How quickly we bounce back reveals our true inherent strength.

Part 2

Business Principles/Practices

Measure Everything

As renowned management guru Peter Ducker says *"what gets measured gets improved."*

Most of the time, as head of the organization, you may be concerned with sales turnover, profit margin, and you may be measuring and monitoring frequently. In today's competitive environment, those measures alone will not be sufficient for sustainable profitability. You need to measure other business and functional parameters. As there are plenty of measures, you can identify and track some of the key performance indicators (KPIs) that are relevant for your business and affect your sustainability.

You can identify the KPIs for performance, quality, delivery, cost, and moral perspectives. Setting KPI and tracking periodically is a time-consuming process, but it rewards you in multiple ways as explained next.

When you start measuring and tracking KPI, you have the following benefits:

- Brings focus
- Makes people aware of their status and enhances accountability
- Improves communication among people
- Enhances people engagement level
- Provides opportunity to make the course correction on time

Initially, you can start with business level KPI and then spread it to a functional level. Eventually, performance management helps you build an organization culture with a winning mindset and competitive advantage.

Discuss the Performance Issues on the Forum

One of the fear phobia most business heads have is conducting the performance review meeting along with the cross-functional team. When the organization is small, one gets information about the performance either by directly being involved or by getting personal information from others on a one-to-one basis. Even when an organization grows regarding product lines, varieties, and turnover and the number of people, the CEO continues using the same tactics of getting information about performance gaps.

This practice may lead to

- Getting different views/responses from different people for the same problem
- Personal time or efficiency loss in cross-checking and taking corrective action
- Lack of accountability at team level on the result

Instead, if you start discussing the performance gap along with the relevant team members in a review meeting forum, you will be likely getting the same response or you can make the team understand the issues in a same perspective.

This kind of forum discussion will bring accountability to the team members and improve your personal efficiency as well.

Set Business Goals with Conviction

Setting the business goals and showing the direction is one of the prime responsibilities of the CEO. Usually it is required to set both business level targets and functional level targets. Business targets can be sales turnover, profits, new products launch, customer addition, etc., and functional level targets can be a rejection cost reduction, manpower productivity, sales target per employee, customer complaint resolution speed, and so on. This classification depends on the nature of the industry and the organization in which you are.

While setting the target, the CEO must have done his homework and set the target with conviction. The target should not be too aspirational and unrealistic, and it must be achievable by the team in with the given time, resource, and capability. Also, the target should not be too lenient with incremental increase as this may not be much motivation for the team to work.

In most of SMEs, we observed the CEO himself would not be convinced about the target, but would push the team by giving them unrealistic targets and sometimes he would be pessimistic about achieving the targets and set them very low. In both cases, the CEO's communication tone and body language would reflect his uncertain mindset to the team.

If the CEO set the target with conviction, he would be more certain about the target and he would drive them by any means to achieve it. Also, his conviction would help to grab the opportunity to meet the target. Also, the team gets motivated when they are working for real, aspirational goals under the visionary leadership.

Invest in Talent

One of the highest returns on investment is investing in people. Competition can copy your technology, process, cost structure, and marketing strategy but it cannot copy your organizational culture. Only people working in the organization along with the head of the organization cultivate the positive, winning culture.

Investing in people consists of four components, namely:

1. Recruit right people for the position at best cost
2. Develop the person's competency on technical, managerial, and behavioral skill

3. Engage them through aspirational organizational targets
4. Empower them for extraordinary performance

It is common in many SMEs to recruit people of any background just to fill the short-term need. This practice creates imbalance in organizational requirement and people capability, which will affect business profitability. While recruiting people, double check that job requirements match with the person's potential and past performance to deliver the result. Enhance your standard of expectation from people and your affordability to pay better to attract the best talents.

Most of the SMEs' CEOs have the wrong belief that providing training and education make the people to leave the organization for a better job opportunity. Remember that if you are not spending your energy, money, and time to develop your people on technical upgradation, managerial skill development, and positive behavioral aspects, people anyhow stay in the organization and deliver lower performance, which is more dangerous for business growth.

One of the research findings on people engagement reveals that people like a challenging environment and look for new learnings from work. People are leaving the organization when they feel that there is less scope for learning and a less challenging environment, even though the pay and benefits are relatively better. Engage your team through shared organizational aspirational goals and empower each one doing their job with freedom and accountability.

Compared to any physical assets, only the human asset is not depreciating as years go by and this is the only asset that brings more returns on investment and profitability to the business. Invest in it!

Improve Your Effectiveness Before Investing

One of the traps most of the SME businesses slip is an increasing overhead due to asset acquisition and utilization. From our experience with hundreds of business owners, they are very enthusiastic in going for expansion when they see the light of opportunities.

When there is indication for new business or incremental volume, the tendency of business owners is to add the capacity even at the cost of borrowing. While it may be logical to go for investment when the opportunity comes in, the hidden fact is that the existing equipment or facilities are not even effectively utilized, 85% as a rule of thumb for capacity utilization in manufacturing industries. Without effectively utilizing the current asset and adding new assets with the same efficiency loss, the business overhead would become fat.

If the business environment is flourishing, the cost can be absorbed, but if the business is in recession or even the competition is aggressive on pricing, your cost structure will not be attractive in the market. You will be losing the opportunity and your internal cost will go up.

So the next time you think about investment in capacity or facility, think twice to ensure that you are effectively utilizing the existing assets. *Your focus must be making the most out of your existing assets before going for further investment.*

Be Lean on the Cost Structure

One of the key reasons the business struggles with profitability or loss is its inability to keep the cost structure lean. Lean cost structure means incurring the expenses that are essentially required and eliminating unnecessary cost elements or low return expenses. Each expense in the organization must have a reasonable rate of return. Waste or unnecessary expenses make the cost structure very fat and overall product cost becomes uncompetitive in the market especially in the buyer's market.

Approaches to keep the cost structure lean are as follows:

1. Track each expense
2. Get convinced about each expense and its return on investment
3. Set the cost efficiency target for each cost element
4. Continually look for waste elimination opportunities through lean system thinking

Regardless of your line of business and monopolistic market or leadership in industry, it is constantly more beneficial to concentrate on saving the cost structure lean, which may be useful during bad times. High growth organization has these practices as their organizational culture.

Systematic Daily Management (SDM) for Assuring Annual Growth

One of the success attributes of successful people is doing the right things on a daily basis. This consistency in small areas would bring big results eventually. Daily management determines your growth annually. If you are not doing right on a daily basis, there is no guarantee for results on a weekly basis, monthly basis, quarterly basis, biannual, and ultimately on an annual basis.

Daily management includes reviewing the previous day's organizational performance of sales, delivery, and customer complaints, and briefly meeting the key people in a forum. This practice would bring many benefits, for example, you can bring the deviation under control immediately and you have more response time to take corrective action. Also, your team is aligned with your way of daily management of things in their respective areas. That way organizational culture is built on the plan "do – check – act" and the path of continuous improvement.

Also, *the habit of managing things on a daily basis or daily management will improve your personal efficiency and you can save more time for the long-term growth of the organization. You become the master of your time.*

Do Not Delegate Your Prime Responsibility to Others

Irrespective of your workload or other priorities, you are accountable for some of the organizational activities and results which you cannot completely delegate to others. Most of the organizations lose the competitive edge not because of a second level management team, but due to the delegation of the CEO's prime responsibility to down the level and not review regularly.

The following activities must be in your agenda on a periodical basis either monthly or weekly or daily, depending upon the size of your business:

1. Month-wise profit and loss trend status and corrective action monitoring
2. Customer's wise satisfaction feedback and delivery performance
3. Setting the growth direction and reviewing the action plan
4. Internal employee engagement level
5. Managing external stakeholder interest
6. Compliance of statutory requirements and overview

The preceding activities require your attention, competency, and decision making on time, which you cannot expect from others just by delegating and not reviewing them on time.

Improve the Effectiveness Before Automation

One of the business traps most of CEOs fall into is automating the equipment, facilities, or operations before improving the effectiveness of the same. Effectiveness is an integrated measure of how you are utilizing your facility, how efficiently you are running your facility, and what is the quality of your product/service. In the manufacturing perspective, it is defined as OPE/OEE – Overall plant or equipment effectiveness. It is a measure of plant/equipment utilization, people productivity, and product quality. Ideally, it can be greater than 85%. When your facility attains an OEE greater than 85, it is time for automating the equipment or adding investment for upgradation, etc.

When the equipment itself is operating at lower OEE, whatever automation or upgradation you add would also be running at the same effectiveness, and in turn the investment will to add your overheads only.

The same approach is applicable for automating business processes like ERP (Enterprise resource planning). Before investing into the ERP system, you need to ensure that you well organize your facility regarding orderliness and higher utilization, people efficiency, and product or service quality. In the absence of basic effectiveness, any automation may not bring much value addition to your bottom line or engagement.

Hence, ensure the fundamental process is in place before going for automation!

Improve Communication and Create a Forum

In professional life, we struggle to meet the expectations of others or others do not live up to our expectations probably due to our inability to clearly express our requirement. Clearly expressing our requirements is the art of communication and developing this skill is a lifelong effort, as we need to deal with different people, with different situations, and we are all at different levels of maturity.

One technique you can use in a professional environment is PURPOSEFUL COMMUNICATION. In purposeful communication technique, one has to communicate with others by briefing the purpose. As human being, we are inherently curious for reasoning. For example, when you ask for any details or analysis from

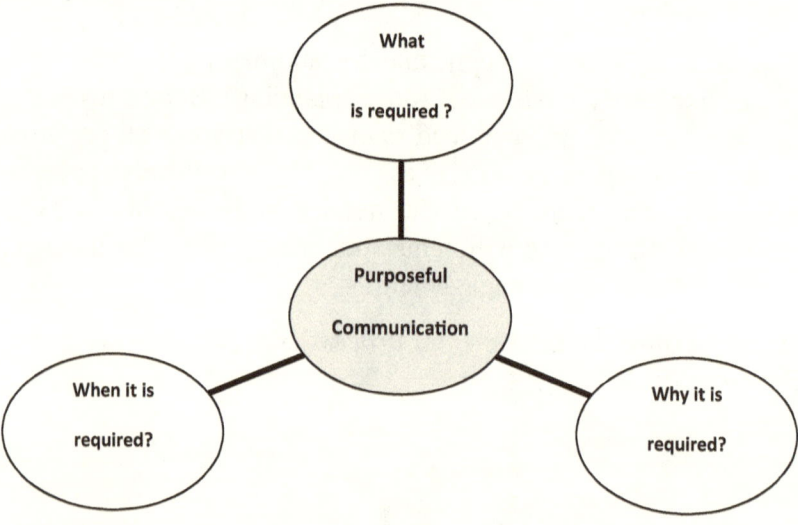

your team, you can go one step further by explaining why you need the data or analysis, when exactly you need it, and how this data or analysis would be useful to you and the organization. By explaining this in detail, we respect others as individuals and there is likely less chance for misunderstanding the expectation.

Moreover, developing the skill of giving the right feedback at the right time to others when things are not going as per our expectations helps correct the situation as well as improve the relationship. Similarly, you can develop the EGO-free attitude for asking feedback from others when you are not clear on the communication or expectations of others.

In an organizational setup, creating multiple forums for communication is one of the responsibilities of the organization head. The forum could be daily meetings, weekly reviews, monthly gatherings, formation of cross-functional teams, small group activities, implementing structured visual management processes across the organization, etc. This structured, well-thought out process of creating communication forums will improve communication among the employees as well as increase the engagement.

Continuous Process Disruption as a Way of Life

On the personal and business front, sometimes we get upset with the pace of growth. We expect different results while we do the same kind of activities or adhere to the same business processes. For continuous growth progress, what is required is *continuous process disruption.*

When we say process disruption, it is not going away from the fundamental process adherence, which would be a disaster even for survival or the existing growth. Process disruption is challenging the existing mindset or process that is producing the current result and continuously inculcating new thinking and new processes for high-level growth. If we do the same thing, we get the same result. If we change the process, at least we can expect different results.

You might have seen some organizations exist more than decades in the same line of products from inception to now that have grown multifold not because of a diversified product line but due to process disruption or continuous innovation in how they manage the business processes.

In business, challenging the existing process and continuously upgrading it, you can expect a different result or a high growth.

On the personal front, by continuously challenging your thinking process you can solicit new opportunities and growth.

The point is that if you want great results, your process also needs to be different. You cannot expect major changes in your result with the same level of process. Continuous process disruption is the only way for sustainable growth!

The question you need to ask yourself is whether you have created an internal environment for continuous process disruption as a way of life.

Build an Environment and Process for Employee Engagement

One of the most fundamental reasons for a consistent growth organization is people and how they are engaging themselves toward the organizational goal. Developing people and bringing them together is the primary responsibility of the CEO or head of the organization.

Bringing the "emotional connection within" is a challenging task, but is possible with two factors. One is creating a positive environment in the organization and the second is establishing a structured, consistent process.

The environmental factor consists of providing basic amenities to the employees, visual managements, and housekeeping through daily management. A positive environment triggers a positive behavior, action, and results among the employees.

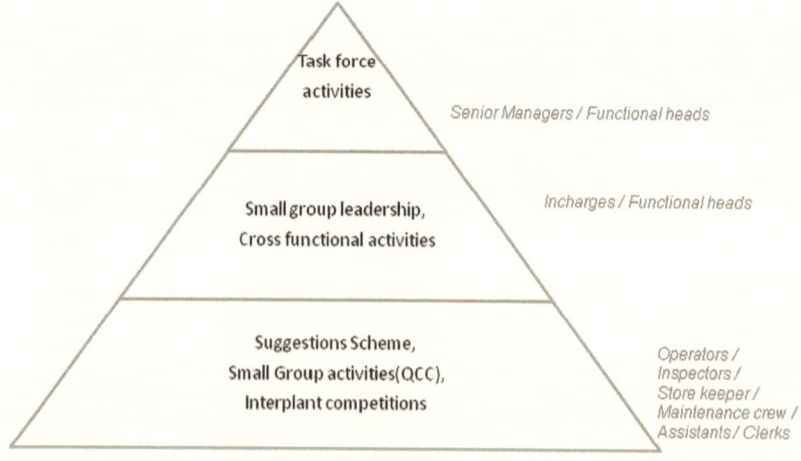

The structured, consistent process includes identifying the engagement methodology for different levels of peoples, defining the administration of engagement initiatives, rewards, recognition plan, etc.

Given in the following text is the framework of employee engagement initiatives for different levels.

Part 3

Business Process Checklist

Operations Management Checklist

1. Do you know the critical equipment/processes that are affecting your overall production delivery schedule?
2. Do you have performance metrics in the critical equipment/process to track the effectiveness on a daily basis?
3. Have you leveled your production rate equally on all the days?
4. Do you know your existing capacity utilization index?
5. Are you seeing a reduction trend in your delivery lead-time?
6. Are you taking measures to reduce your lead-time compared to last year?
7. Are you meeting 100% delivery actualization for all customers?
8. Do you have a measure for inventory?
9. Are you tracking OEE measure in your critical machine/manufacturing line on a daily basis?
10. Are you tracking changeover loss from one customer product to another?
11. Are you tracking rejection cost for each customer?
12. Is there reduction trend in rejection cost for each customer?
13. Are you tracking equipment downtime loss every day?
14. Do you have a system to review your operations performance on a daily basis?
15. Is your operation's team aware of DAILY PRODUCTION TARGET?
16. Does your team practice structured problem-solving methodologies, tools, and techniques?

17. Is your plant layout helping you improve the material/communication flow?
18. Are you tracking safety incidence on a daily basis?
19. Is your team aware of safety practices in mechanical/electrical/fire hazardous prevention and detection?
20. Are you tracking the cost of quality in your organization?

Strategic Focus Checklist

1. Do you have growth plan for next 3 years?
2. Are you spending 30–40% of your time on growth and developmental aspects than operational issues?
3. Do you have factory master plans for 3–5 years?
4. Are you depending on one customer or industry too heavily?
5. Do you have diversification across industry customers/demographic customer base?
6. Do you have a broad succession plan at your level?
7. Do you have clarity to increase our profitability or sales turnover?
8. Have you ever evaluated your business risk?
9. Have you initiated lean system thinking in your organization?
10. Have you identified your core competency and nurtured the same?

People Development Checklist

1. Have you assessed your organization talent mapping?
2. Do you have an organizational structure with clear roles and responsibilities?
3. Do you have a competency mapping of your employees?
4. Do you have plans for the development of your employees, at least for those in critical positions?
5. Do you have any engagement initiatives in your organization?
6. Do you measure attrition/absenteeism as your priority measures?
7. Do you have a communication forum with your team?
8. Have you created a conducive environment for the team to experiment or to take risks?
9. Have you systematically created a process for recruitment?
10. Do you have a system or process to capture the employee's voice about the organization?

Sales Management Checklist

1. Are you tracking sales performance for each customer for every month/quarterly/annually?
2. Do you have a sales target for each month and have you communicated it to them?
3. Do you have a lost sales order analysis every month?
4. Do you have a standard policy on pricing decision and estimation?
5. Do you have a single point contact for customer order handling?
6. Do you compare your intended profitability and achieved profitability for each customer?
7. Do you have a structured process to execute the sales order on time and cost?
8. Do you have strategy for improving sales performance for each customer based on volume and value proposition?
9. Do you have the next 3 months' sales forecasts and order fulfillment plans in common platform?
10. Do you have a forum to discuss the sales' operational performance together?

Finance Management Checklist

1. Are you tracking your profit and loss every month?
2. Are you tracking your expenses in each category of customers/functions/processes?
3. Do you have organizational initiatives to reduce the cost?
4. Do you track inventory every month?
5. Are you regularly calibrating your system vs. physical stock inventory?
6. Do you have key ratio metrics for your business operations?
7. Do you have a budget for each process/plant/functions/customer-specific expenses?
8. Do you know your breakeven point for your business operations?
9. Do you have exclusive KPIs for cost and profitability areas?
10. Have you identified and made accountable anyone on statutory compliance on time and quality?

New Product Development/Marketing/Customer Service

1. Are you meeting your customer's specified development time in your new product development?
2. Do you have project management practices in your new product development process?
3. Do you have a dedicated team for value creation activities?
4. Do you have a reliable, consistent plan to reach out to new customers?
5. Do you have any measure to evaluate the success of developmental efforts?
6. Are you responding to your potential customer's query within 2 days' time?
7. Do you have an exclusive team to manage the customer's requirement or expectations?
8. Do you have a development or marketing budget in your organization?
9. Do you have an updated website?
10. Do you track development expenses exclusively?
11. Do you have practices of adding value to customer's design/material or processes?
12. Do you have a structured and informal process to get the customer's feedback about your product and services?

Part 4

Overview about Important Management Concepts, Tools, and Techniques

OVERALL EQUIPMENT EFFECTIVENESS

Overall Equipment Effectivess (OEE) is one of the performance measures to assess the effectiveness of your critical equipment or manufacturing line. Through this one measure, you shall holistically understand the utilization, people efficiency and quality of the product. OEE is one of the simple and most powerful operational excellence measure for any organization.

ABC ANALYSIS

ABC analysis helps to put the different control mechanisms of your inventory. This analysisi helps to classify your inventory into high-value consumption items, low-value consummation items, and medium-value consumption items. Based on the classification, you can implement different inventory control measures like norm settings, storage quantity, ordering frequency, reporting and reviews, etc.

CAUSE ANALYSIS

For any problem, there could be many causes contributing to the effect. This root cause analysis helps to list down all the possible causes in structured formats and then validate each cause, filtering the possible causes into probable causes and each probable cause going in-depth to understand the root. Some of the tools and techniques used in root cause analysis are brainstorming, cause and effect diagram, and why–why analysis.

TOTAL EMPLOYEE ENGAGEMENT

Total Employee Engagement is a concept to involve or engage all the employees toward contributing to the organizational goal. Each level of employees needs different engagement and motivation and their contribution level toward an organizational goal is different, which involves designing and executing various engagement drives, forums, initiatives, rewards, recognition, etc. Some of the popular engagement initiatives are suggestion schemes, small group activities, and cross-functional team participation.

SMALL GROUP ACTIVITIES

As part of total employee engagement, in these small group activities, employees are encouraged to form a team to solve particular organizational problems, plan and execute the solutions to the problem, get recognition, and dissolve the team. Primarily, it is targeted at front line operators and administrators to resolve the problems relating to their work areas. Most of the small group activities use simple, structured problem-solving methodologies, tools, and techniques under the guidance of a leader.

KEY PERFORMANCE INDICATORS

In a organization, you could be performing many activities.But at the end of the day, only a few activities and their effectiveness matter to organizational profitability and growth. This KPI as the term itself implies identifies important parameters at the business level and the functional level. Those parameters are specified with the right unit of measure, current level, and desired target level.

QUICK CHANGEOVER TECHNIQUES

One of the wastes in any manufacturing or service system is time loss due to changeover from one product type to another. This changeover loss can take place in machines like die setting, tool settings, comp replenishment in assembly, and so on. Changeover loss is the time loss between producing the last pieces of product A and the first good piece of product B. This changeover loss is significant in certain manufacturing or service systems. This quick changeover technique comes with a structured way of organizing the changeover process. Some of the concepts are single-minute exchange of dies (SMED) and one-touch exchange of dies (OTED).

STRUCTURED PROBLEM-SOLVING METHODOLOGIES

There is a tendency to solve the problem is to quick fix with temporary solutions and move on and again at later stage, work on the same problem as firefighting mindset. The structured problem-solving methodologies come with a systematic process of solving any problem with permanent solutions approach. The typical steps include defining the problem, data collection, prioritization, analysis of causes, root cause analysis, defining action plan, implementing the action plan, checking the results, and then again taking counter measures until reaching the desired solution.

There are various methodologies and approaches available to solve problems like six sigma approach, 8D, and traditional problem solving using QC tools and techniques. Fundamentally, all the methodologies use the P-D-C-A approach only.

PARETO PRINCIPLE

This principle is also known as the 80/20 rule for approaching any problem. It is based on the assumption that roughly 80% of the effects come from 20% of the causes. This principle can be applied to any problems like revenue maximization, cost reduction, quality improvement, etc.

MISTAKE PROOFING TECHNIQUES

In any human work, there is chance for making errors. These mistake proofing techniques aim to prevent the error at the source or at least detect the error after it occurred so that it would not be passed on to the next stage or the customer. This technique comes with different ideas to prevent or detect the error at the source. This technique can be applied to any environment where there is scope for human error.

VISUAL MANAGEMENT

One of the powerful concepts in management is visual management. It consists of visual display, visual metrics, and visual controls. Effective planning and implementation of visual management systems helps improve communication, expose problems, and solve them at the right time, improving people engagement across the organization. It can be applied in both manufacturing and service areas.

PRINCIPLES OF ERGONOMICS

One of the micro-productivity tools is an application of ergonomics. This discipline mainly concerns the human–work relationship. It focuses primarily on optimizing the four factors like person, tool, work, and environment.

TALENT MAPPING

Talent mapping is one of the strategic and tactic tools for people development. It will help map people on a potential and performance basis and will also help diagnose the organizational person's strengths to prepare the development plan for the individual. This mapping requires a high level of maturity and judgment.

COMPETENCY MAPPING

One of the tools is to assess and map the skill, knowledge, and behavior requirement for a particular position and the existing incumbent level. This mapping will help develop the competency of the individual through either online or offline training, coaching, mentoring, etc.

VALUE STREAM MAPPING (VSM)

This lean visualization technique will help map the entire supply chain process from end to end. VSM will help to see the current state of the material flow, process flow, and information flow across the organization. It also helps identify the waste elimination or reduction opportunities at the big picture level. VSM can be used as a blueprint for future improvements of organizational supply chain activities. Mapping is must before starting any lean initiatives in the organization.

PROJECT MANAGEMENT

Other than operational activities, all activities can be considered as a project. The project management discipline deals with a set of techniques, methodologies to plan and execute the projects to achieve planned, on time execution, planned quality achievements, and planned cost targets. The knowledge, tools, and techniques of project management can be applied for new product development, new plant expansion, or any new management change initiatives.

COST OF QUALITY

Cost of Quality is one of the holistic measures of cost associated with product and service quality in the organization. This measure helps to see the cost associated with quality in different perspectives and helps to drive the organization holistically on improving the quality on each stage rather than looking at the cost of quality in isolated functions or areas.

MAINTENANCE MANAGEMENT

This management is all about the effective usage of assets like machinery and utilities. This covers the aspects of breakdown maintenance, preventive maintenance, planned maintenance, empowering the operators to own the equipment, spares management, reliability maintenance, etc.

QUALITY ASSURANCE

Quality assurance is all about ensuring quality built at each stage of product development and manufacturing process rather than controlling the quality at each stage. It is more about engineering, problem solving at source, culture building on continuous improvement, and proactive management than reactive management.

INVENTORY TURN

Inventory Turn is one of the basic measures of inventory management. It measures the efficiency of the inventory level about the organizational sales level. It is measured as the ratio of sales quantity to the average inventory level at a given time. This measure helps to track how efficiently management rotates the inventory stock about sales.

BREAK EVEN ANALYSIS

Break even analysis is important to plan your finance and cost management. The breakeven point is when you get neither profit nor loss, and beyond breakeven you generate positive cash flow or profit. This analysis is required whenever you are planning for expansion, new product introduction, or even in your existing business. This analysis will help to plan your production or sales, expenses, and even your working capital.

LOST ORDER ANALYSIS

Lost order analysis is all about analyzing past orders, which you lost to competition. This analysis on a frequent basis will help you to get new insight on competition, pricing, and internal flexibility and from that learning you can change your strategy and tactics to convert potential customers into regular ones.

FLOW MANUFACTURING

Flow manufacturing is one of the lean manufacturing concepts, where you convert RM (Raw material) into FG (Finished goods) with minimal or no delay in the flow. Single piece flow is one of the idealistic measures of flow manufacturing. To bring the idealistic state of single piece flow, you need to improve on the imbalance factor in your production rate, rejection control, equipment utilization, work standardization, plant layout improvement, communication improvement, etc. The ultimate business measure is lead-time reduction from the day you receive the order to fulfilling the order to the customer.

LINE BALANCING

One of the flow manufacturing techniques is balancing the production line or cell with regard to takt time or customer pace.

TAKT TIME

TAKT time is the defined time at which the customer is expecting his product to be produced. For example, if takt time is 1 min, the customer is expecting the product to be rolled out every minute. Accordingly, you need to balance your entire manufacturing process to within 1 min.

LEAD TIME

Lead time is the time the system takes to deliver the product or service from the moment you receive the order to deliver to the customer. It comprises both value-added and non-value added activities. This lead-time reduction must be one of your KPIs as it reflects the system efficiency in totality.

CYCLE TIME

Cycle time is the time taken to produce one item. It consists of value-added time. Your focus must be on reducing the process cycle time if it is constrained for delivery.

CHANGEOVER TIME

Change over time represents the time elapsed between the good products produced from comp 1 and the good products produced from comp 2. It includes setting tools/dies and adjustments of equipment or tools to achieve the quality required for the product.

PRODUCT VS. PROCESS LAYOUT

The way the plant equipment and processes are organized in terms of process or product layout has major implication on your material flow, lead time, and information flow. The plant layout has to be reloaded depending on the product varieties and volume.

HOUSEKEEPING PRINCIPLES

The fundamental of operational excellence is keeping the house in order. The important principles of housekeeping are as follows:

- Keep what you need
- Provide a location for each part

- Provide identification for each part
- Establish a process for cleaning and sustaining

FAILURE MODE EFFECT ANALYSIS (FMEA)

FMEA is one of the quality assurance tools that can be used for existing and new designs and processes. It is looking at the risk associated with the design or process from the customer's perspective. The risk can be primarily related to quality and safety. This tool can be used in design, process, and service area as well.

STATISTICAL PROCESS CONTROL (SPC)

Statistical process control is a method of quality control, which uses statistical methods to monitor and control a process. SPC can be applied in any manufacturing process where the process parameter can be measured against the target specification. SPC can be taught to the operators people and the quality can be controlled at source.

CONTROL CHARTS

Control charts are SPC tools used to determine if a manufacturing or business process is in a state of control or not. There are various types of control charts depending on the process observation type, namely, variables and attributes. Control chart can be taught to the operators and quality can be controlled at source.

GANTT CHART

Gantt chart is a simple visual tool that shows the plan vs. the actual status of any activity at any given time. It can be used for tracking the progress of actions in the project environment as well as in an operational environment.

WHY–WHY ANALYSIS

One of the techniques to find the root cause of the problem is why–why analysis. In this method, each probable cause will be questioned to a deeper level to get the root cause of the problem.

FACTORY MASTER PLAN (FMP)

The factory master plan is a strategic planning process in which you plan your future business, say 3–5 years' timeline from all perspectives. FMP will help plan your resources like finance, people, capability improvement, etc. This plan is a dynamic process and needs to be done periodically.

LEAN MANUFACTURING

The lean manufacturing system can be understood by relating to the human body. If the person appears "lean", then the general assumption is that he/she is free from unnecessary FAT in the body, hence free from unnecessary side-effects like BP, joint pain, laziness, etc. The person is perceived as healthy, more flexible, active, etc.

In the same way, lean manufacturing means the manufacturing system is free from unnecessary fats like high inventory, high rejection, high breakdowns or line stoppage factors, etc., which lead to more flexibility in delivery, less lead time, first time right, low cost of manufacturing, free flow of communication, etc.

LEAN SYSTEM THINKING

A lean system or lean organization is free from unnecessary waste in the entire value chain starting from the extended supply chain system to the customer, even after the sales service system.

Lean system thinking is more than the application of tools and techniques.

It is a culture of continuous improvement or a way of working or winning the mindset of everyone working for the organization.

VALUE CHAIN ANALYSIS

This is one of the management initiatives to understand the cost stack-up in each product and analyze the opportunity to take out the cost through kaizen, process improvement, waste elimination or reduction, material yield improvements, supply chain initiatives, etc.

PRODUCT PRICING ANALYSIS

This is a systematic analysis of cost stack-up in product cost and identifying the opportunity for cost takeout without affecting the customer's deliverables.

SWOT ANALYSIS (SWOT)

SWOT Analysis is a systematic assessment of organizational strength, weakness, opportunity, and threat from the marketing, product, people, and resource points of view. This analysis is strategic, dynamic process and needs to be done periodically by the senior leadership team.

Additional Resources

For Business transformation insights, concepts, tools, and techniques, please visit
    http://businesstransformationinsights.blogspot.in/

For a PowerPoint presentation on business transformation concepts, tools, and techniques, please visit
    http://www.slideshare.net/ganeshbabu7

For more insight on personal and business growth, please visit
    https://www.youtube.com/channel/UCtRJ5g7OD5sCTke3kPAr9mg

Expression of my Gratitude

This book is the outcome of all my experiences and learnings from all the human lives that touched me in one way or another and inspired me. It is my duty to acknowledge all and it is difficult to mention all them all. I sincerely convey my gratitude to all the souls.

However, I would like to mention a few of them who significantly influenced my life. To my mother Meena who has given me a good value system by living and demonstrating. To my father Shanmugam who demonstrated to live a balanced life and to lead a prosperous one. His blessing before the last breath is guiding me forever. To my sister Malathi and her family for their love and affection. To my brother-in-laws for their moral support and all relatives for giving me a sense of belonging. I need to mention about my wife Thaiyal Nayagi for her caring and support to pursue my passion through Winning Minds Solutions. I feel so gifted to have my son Raghav who makes me smile and gives hope of the future.

I remember and convey my sincere gratitude to all my teachers who taught me subjects as well as molded me to what I am today. I am gifted to have those selfless teachers in my life who have taken enormous interest and effort to shape me. I am here today because of my teachers.

I thank the divine power to shower its blessings on me to study in prominent institutions and to work with great organizations that made all the differences in my thinking processes and perspectives.

My special thanks to my associate Vijaya Kumar for his excellent work on image designing.

I convey my gratitude to all my bosses from whom I learned different ways of managing the challenges. They have mentored me in many tough occasions with their insights.

Last but not least, I thank all my clients, especially the business heads who have given me the opportunity to learn more about business management. I dedicate this book to those business heads who are striving for excellence in their business.

About the Author: Ganesh Babu

S. Ganesh Babu is Founder and CEO of Winning Minds Solutions, an organization that helps individual and organizations to reach the next level of growth. Ganesh is an industrial engineering graduate from Guindy Engineering College with 21 years' contribution in various functions, namely, industrial engineering, manufacturing systems, operations, and project management in leading group companies like TVS, Murugappa group in India. Lastly, he served as general manager in Whirlpool, India.

His core expertise areas are lean manufacturing, process/industrial engineering, plant layout, material handling, new product development through project management, and people development. Since 2012, his organization Winning Minds Solutions has so far helped more than 40 **SME organizations** to improve productivity, business profitability, and build a performance-based culture to sustain business profitability.

Some of his clients include corporates like Tube Investment of India, Larsen & Toubro (L&T), Rane Brake Linings, Asian Paints, Apollo Tyres, Maini Group, Essae group companies, and SMEs like Dimo Castings, Southern Pressure Castings, Vijay Spheroidals, and Bright Brothers.

As a certified project management professional and lean system thinking expert, he has conducted technical and managerial workshops in both corporate and public forums that produced significant results on shift in mindset and business results.

Passionate about the development of people, his flagship coaching programs **"Personal Success Coaching"** for student development into business executive and **"Life Excellence"** for adults to manage life with a balanced growth are creating an impact on more than 12,500 people so far.

As a certified performance coach, he is regularly writing articles on life excellence in educational magazines and websites. He is the author of the book **"Thoughts on Life Excellence."**

www.ingramcontent.com/pod-product-compliance
Lightning Source LLC
Chambersburg PA
CBHW031114180526
45163CB00013B/2958